MASTERPIECES OF PIANO MUSIC
WOLFGANG AMADEUS MOZART

Amsco Publications
New York/London/Sydney/Cologne

International Standard Book Number: 0.8256.2423.1

Exclusive Distributors:
Music Sales Corporation
24 East 22nd Street, New York, NY 10010 USA
Music Sales Limited
8/9 Frith Street, London W1V 5TZ England
Music Sales Pty. Limited
120 Rothschild Street, Rosebery, Sydney, NSW 2018, Australia

Printed in the United States of America by
Vicks Lithograph and Printing Corporation

Sonata *in A Major, K.331.*

W. A. Mozart (Köchel No. 331)

Andante grazioso.

Var. I.

Var. II.

Var. III.
Minore.

Var. V.
Adagio.

Var. VI.
Allegro.

(Menuetto D.C.)

Alla Turca.
Allegretto.

Sonata *in C Major, K.545.*

Rondo (Allegro)

12 Variations on *Ah! vous dirai-je, maman, K.265.*

Theme

VAR. VIII
Minore

VAR. IX
Maggiore

12 Variations on *La Belle Françoise.*

Theme
Andante quasi Allegretto

VAR. IV

Adagio Tempo I.

VAR. VII

VAR. VIII

VAR. IX
Minore

VAR. X
Maggiore

VAR. XI
Adagio

VAR. XII
Presto

Tempo I.

Rondo *in D Major, K.485.*

Sonata *in Eb Major, K.282.*

Adagio

Coda

Minuetto I

Minuetto II (Trio)

Minuetto 1. da capo

Allegro

Sonata *in G Major,* K.283.

64

Andante

Presto

Fantasy *in D minor, K.397.*

Sonata *in D Major, K.311.*

Allegro con spirito

Andante con espressione

Rondo
Allegro

89

12 Variations on *The Romanza Je Suis Lindor, K.354.*

Theme
Allegretto

VAR. I

VAR. II

VAR. III

VAR. V

VAR. VI

VAR. VII
Maestoso

VAR. VIII
Minore

VAR. X

VAR. XI
Molto adagio

VAR. XII
Tempo di Menuetto

10 Variations from Gluck's opera,
Pilgrime von Mecca, K.455.

Theme
Allegretto

VAR. II

VAR. III

VAR. IV

VAR. V
Minore

VAR. VI
Maggiore

VAR. VII

VAR. VIII

VAR. IX
Adagio

VAR. X
Allegro

Fantasy and Fugue *in C Major, K.394.*

Tempo I.

Fuge

Andante maestoso

Sonata *in D Major, K.284.*

Rondeau en Polonaise
Andante

Theme
Andante

Var. II

Var. III

Var. IV

Var. V

Var. VI

Var. IX

Var. X

Var. XI.
Adagio cantabile

Var. XII

Allegro

Andante *in F Major for small organ, K.616.*

Adagio *In B minor, K.540.*

A Little Gigue *In C Major, K.574.*

Menuetto *In D Major,* K.355.

9 Variations *on a Minuet* by J.P. Duport.

VAR. II

VAR. III

172

VAR. V

VAR. VI
Minore

VAR. VII
Maggiore

VAR. VIII
Adagio

12 Variations *on a Minuet* by J.C. Fischer, *K.179.*

Theme

VAR. I

VAR. II

VAR. III

VAR. IV

VAR. V

VAR. VI

VAR. VII

VAR. VIII

VAR. IX

VAR. X

VAR. XII
Allegro